BOOKS BY MARK STRAND

POEMS

The Story of Our Lives   *1973*
The Sargeantville Notebook (pamphlet)   *1973*
Darker   *1970*   ·
Reasons for Moving   *1968*
Sleeping with One Eye Open   *1964*

TRANSLATIONS

The Owl's Insomnia
(SELECTED POEMS OF RAPHAEL ALBERTI)   *1973*
18 Poems from the Quechua   *1971*

THE
STORY
OF OUR
LIVES

THE
STORY
OF OUR
LIVES

Poems by

MARK STRAND

Atheneum

NEW YORK

1973

The poems have appeared in the following periodicals:

THE AMERICAN REVIEW: *Inside the Story*
THE COMEDY OF ART (catalog accompanying the exhibition of Toulouse-Lautrec
   lithographs at Boston University): *She*
FIELD: *Elegy for My Father*
THE NEW YORKER: *The Room* and *The Story of Our Lives*
THE OHIO REVIEW: *In Celebration*
POETRY: *The Untelling*
THE SATURDAY REVIEW: *To Begin*

The author wishes to acknowledge his gratitude to the trustees of Yaddo, where
some of this book was written.

CONTENTS

I   ELEGY FOR MY FATHER

II   THE ROOM

III   THE STORY OF OUR LIVES

I

ELEGY
FOR
MY FATHER

ELEGY FOR MY FATHER
(*Robert Strand 1908-68*)

1   *The Empty Body*

The hands were yours, the arms were yours,
But you were not there.
The eyes were yours, but they were closed and would not open.
The distant sun was there.
The moon poised on the hill's white shoulder was there.
The wind on Bedford Basin was there.
The pale green light of winter was there.
Your mouth was there,
But you were not there.
When somebody spoke, there was no answer.
Clouds in the blind air came down
And buried the buildings along the water,
And the water was silent.
The gulls stared.
The years, the hours, that would not find you
Turned in the wrists of others.
There was no pain. It had gone.
There were no secrets. There was nothing to say.
The shade scattered its ashes.
The body was yours, but you were not there.
The air shivered against its skin.
The dark leaned into its eyes.
But you were not there.

2 *Answers*

Why did you travel?
Because the house was cold.
Why did you travel?
Because it is what I have always done between sunset and sunrise.
What did you wear?
I wore a blue suit, a white shirt, yellow tie, and yellow socks.
What did you wear?
I wore nothing. A scarf of pain kept me warm.
Who did you sleep with?
I slept with a different woman each night.
Who did you sleep with?
I slept alone. I have always slept alone.
Why did you lie to me?
I always thought I told the truth.
Why did you lie to me?
Because the truth lies like nothing else and I love the truth.
Why are you going?
Because nothing means much to me anymore.
Why are you going?
I don't know. I have never known.
How long shall I wait for you?
Do not wait for me. I am tired and I want to lie down.
Are you tired and do you want to lie down?
Yes, I am tired and I want to lie down.

3   *Your Dying*

Nothing could stop you.
Not the best day. Not the quiet. Not the ocean rocking.
You went on with your dying.
Not the trees
Under which you walked, not the trees that shaded you.
Not the doctor
Who warned you, the white-haired young doctor who saved you
  once.
You went on with your dying.
Nothing could stop you. Not your son. Not your daughter
Who fed you and made you into a child again.
Not your son who thought you would live forever.
Not the wind that shook your lapels.
Not the stillness that offered itself to your motion.
Not your shoes that grew heavier.
Not your eyes that refused to look ahead.
Nothing could stop you.
You sat in your room and stared at the city
And went on with your dying.
You went to work and let the cold enter your clothes.
You let blood seep into your socks.
Your face turned white.
Your voice cracked in two.
You leaned on your cane.
But nothing could stop you.
Not your friends who gave you advice.
Not your son. Not your daughter who watched you grow small.
Not fatigue that lived in your sighs.
Not your lungs that would fill with water.
Not your sleeves that carried the pain of your arms.

Nothing could stop you.
You went on with your dying.
When you played with children you went on with your dying.
When you sat down to eat,
When you woke up at night, wet with tears, your body sobbing,
You went on with your dying.
Nothing could stop you.
Not the past.
Not the future with its good weather.
Not the view from your window, the view of the graveyard.
Not the city. Not the terrible city with its wooden buildings.
Not defeat. Not success.
You did nothing but go on with your dying.
You put your watch to your ear.
You felt yourself slipping.
You lay on the bed.
You folded your arms over your chest and you dreamed of the
    world without you,
Of the space under the trees,
Of the space in your room,
Of the spaces that would now be empty of you,
And you went on with your dying.
Nothing could stop you.
Not your breathing. Not your life.
Not the life you wanted.
Not the life you had.
Nothing could stop you.

4   *Your Shadow*

You have your shadow.

The places where you were have given it back.

The hallways and bare lawns of the orphanage have given it back.

The Newsboys Home has given it back.

The streets of New York have given it back and so have the streets of Montreal.

The rooms in Belém where lizards would snap at mosquitos have given it back.

The dark streets of Manaus and the damp streets of Rio have given it back.

Mexico City where you wanted to leave it has given it back.

And Halifax where the harbor would wash its hands of you has given it back.

You have your shadow.

When you traveled the white wake of your going sent your shadow below, but when you arrived it was there to greet you. You had your shadow.

The doorways you entered lifted your shadow from you and when you went out, gave it back. You had your shadow.

Even when you forgot your shadow, you found it again; it had been with you.

Once in the country the shade of a tree covered your shadow and you were not known.

Once in the country you thought your shadow had been cast by somebody else. Your shadow said nothing.

Your clothes carried your shadow inside; when you took them off, it spread like the dark of your past.

And your words that float like leaves in an air that is lost, in a place no one knows, gave you back your shadow.

Your friends gave you back your shadow.

Your enemies gave you back your shadow. They said it was heavy and would cover your grave.

Your wife took your shadow and said she would keep it; she died and you found it beside you on the bed.

You hated the sun because in the morning it would take your shadow and at night would give it back unused, untouched.

The night was good because it was your shadow and you were large surrounding the moon.

Winter took your shadow which lay like a long cape on the snow and gave it back with your breath.

When you died your shadow slept at the mouth of the furnace and ate ashes for bread.

It rejoiced among ruins.

It watched while others slept.

It shone like crystal among the tombs.

It composed itself like air.

It wanted to be like snow on water.

It wanted to be nothing, but that was not possible.

It came to my house.

It sat on my shoulders.

Your shadow is yours. I told it so. I said it was yours.

I have carried it with me too long. I give it back.

5   *Mourning*

They mourn for you.
When you rise at midnight,
And the dew glitters on the stone of your cheeks,
They mourn for you.
They lead you back into the empty house.
They carry the chairs and tables inside.
They sit you down and teach you to breathe.
And your breath burns,
It burns the pine box and the ashes fall like sunlight.
They give you a book and tell you to read.
They listen and their eyes fill with tears.
The women stroke your fingers.
They comb the yellow back into your hair.
They shave the frost from your beard.
They knead your thighs.
They dress you in fine clothes.
They rub your hands to keep them warm.
They feed you. They offer you money.
They get on their knees and beg you not to die.
When you rise at midnight they mourn for you.
They close their eyes and whisper your name over and over.
But they cannot drag the buried light from your veins.
They cannot reach your dreams.
Old man, there is no way.
Rise and keep rising, it does no good.
They mourn for you the way they can.

6   The New Year

It is winter and the new year.
Nobody knows you.
Away from the stars, from the rain of light,
You lie under the weather of stones.
There is no thread to lead you back.
Your friends doze in the dark
Of pleasure and cannot remember.
Nobody knows you. You are the neighbor of nothing.
You do not see the rain falling and the man walking away,
The soiled wind blowing its ashes across the city.
You do not see the sun dragging the moon like an echo.
You do not see the bruised heart go up in flames,
The skulls of the innocent turn into smoke.
You do not see the scars of plenty, the eyes without light.
It is over. It is winter and the new year.
The meek are hauling their skins into heaven.
The hopeless are suffering the cold with those who have nothing
    to hide.
It is over and nobody knows you.
There is starlight drifting on the black water.
There are stones in the sea no one has seen.
There is a shore and people are waiting.
And nothing comes back.
Because it is over.
Because there is silence instead of a name.
Because it is winter and the new year.

II

THE ROOM

THE ROOM

I stand at the back of a room
and you have just entered.
I feel the dust
fall from the air
onto my cheeks.
I feel the ice
of sunlight on the walls.
The trees outside
remind me of something
you are not yet aware of.
You have just entered.
There is something like sorrow
in the room.
I believe you think
it has wings
and will change me.
The room is so large
I wonder what you are thinking
or why you have come.
I ask you,
What are you doing?
You have just entered
and cannot hear me.
Where did you buy
the black coat you are wearing?
You told me once.
I cannot remember
what happened between us.
I am here. Can you see me?
I shall lay my words on the table

as if they were gloves,
as if nothing had happened.
I hear the wind
and I wonder what are
the blessings
born of enclosure.
The need to get away?
The desire to arrive?
I am so far away
I seem to be in the room's past
and so much here
the room is beginning
to vanish around me.
It will be yours soon.
You have just entered.
I feel myself drifting,
beginning to be
somewhere else.
Houses are rising
out of my past,
people are walking
under the trees.
You do not see them.
You have just entered.
The room is long.
There is a table in the middle.
You will walk
toward the table,
toward the flowers,
toward the presence of sorrow
which has begun to move
among objects,

its wings beating
to the sound of your heart.
You shall come closer
and I shall begin to turn away.
The black coat you are wearing,
where did you get it?
You told me once
and I cannot remember.
I stand at the back
of the room and I know
if you close your eyes
you will know why
you are here;
that to stand in a space
is to forget time,
that to forget time
is to forget death.
Soon you will take off your coat.
Soon the room's whiteness
will be a skin for your body.
I feel the turning of breath
around what we are going to say.
I know by the way
you raise your hand
you have noticed the flowers
on the table.
They will lie
in the wake of our motions
and the room's map
will lie before us
like a simple rug.
You have just entered.

There is nothing to be done.
I stand at the back of the room
and I believe you see me.
The light consumes the chair,
absorbing its vacancy,
and will swallow itself
and release the darkness
that will fill the chair again.
I shall be gone.
You will say you are here.
I can hear you say it.
I can almost hear you say it.
Soon you will take off your black coat
and the room's whiteness
will close around you
and you will move
to the back of the room.
Your name will no longer be known,
nor will mine.
I stand at the back
and you have just entered.
The beginning is about to occur.
The end is in sight.

SHE

To Bill and Sandy Bailey

She slept without the usual concerns,
the troubling dreams—the pets
moving through the museum,
the carved monsters, the candles
giving themselves up to darkness.
She slept without caring what she looked like,
without considering the woman
who would come or the men who would leave
or the mirrors or the basin of cold water.
She slept on one side, the sheets
pouring into the room's cold air,
the pillow shapeless, her flesh
no longer familiar. Her sleep
was a form of neglect.
She did nothing for days,
the sun and moon had washed up
on the same shore. Her negligee
became her flesh, her flesh became
the soft folding of air over the sheets.
And there was no night, nor any sign of it.
Nothing curled in the air
but the sound of nothing,
the hymn of nothing, the humming
of the room, of its past.
Her flesh turned from itself
into the sheets of light.
She began to wake; her hair spilled
into the rivers of shadow.
Her eyes half-open, she saw the man across the room,
she watched him and could not choose

between sleep and wakefulness.
And he watched her
and the moment became their lives
so that she would never rise or turn from him,
so that he would always be there.

IN CELEBRATION

You sit in a chair, touched by nothing, feeling
the old self become the older self, imagining
only the patience of water, the boredom of stone.
You think that silence is the extra page,
you think that nothing is good or bad, not even
the darkness that fills the house while you sit watching
it happen. You've seen it happen before. Your friends
move past the window, their faces soiled with regret.
You want to wave but cannot raise your hand.
You sit in a chair. You turn to the nightshade spreading
a poisonous net around the house. You taste
the honey of absence. It is the same wherever
you are, the same if the voice rots before
the body, or the body rots before the voice.
You know that desire leads only to sorrow, that sorrow
leads to achievement which leads to emptiness.
You know that this is different, that this
is the celebration, the only celebration,
that by giving yourself over to nothing,
you shall be healed. You know there is joy in feeling
your lungs prepare themselves for an ashen future,
so you wait, you stare and you wait, and the dust settles
and the miraculous hours of childhood wander in darkness.

TO BEGIN

He lay in bed not knowing how to begin.
His mind was unclear, and whatever he felt
faded into an aspect of something
he had known already. Maybe
someone could tell him what to do.
Maybe he could say what he wanted
in his own voice and still be surprised,
say, for example, that it was just before dawn,
that the moon was still a prisoner to stone,
that the sun called so faintly
only a few birds heard it
and they sang for the light
the way some men sing for bread.
If he could say it so that people
believed him, so that he believed it,
he would go on. He would begin
to believe that waking meant
casting his sleep back into the night.
Later, he could learn to say what he meant
without actually saying it.
But he lay in bed, powerless to begin.

He thought how he had always carried
darkness into day where it blazed
into a likeness of himself.
He had stood like a ghost in sunlight,
barely visible, in whose eyes
the trees, the windows, the vanishings
of a previous life became real again.
Maybe he could say that.

But to whom? And for what reason?
To whom could he say that to lose
is to lose something, that to lose
again and again is to have more
and more to lose, that losing is having?

There was no reason to get up.
Let the sun shine without him.
He knew he was not needed,
that his speech was a mirror, at best,
that once he had imagined his words
floating upwards, luminous and threatening,
moving among the stars, becoming the stars,
becoming in the end the equal of all the dead
and the living. He had imagined this
and did not care to again.
If only he could say something,
something that had the precision
of his staying in bed.
It took no courage, no special
recklessness to discredit silence.
He had tried to do it, but had failed.
He had gone to bed and slept.
The phrases had disappeared, sinking
into sleep, unwanted and uncalled for.

He stared at the ceiling
and imagined his breath shaping itself into words.
He imagined that he would go to the water and look down,
that he would see the shimmer of fish
over the ruinous coral
and watch them die in the shade of his image.

21

But he could never say that.
Maybe the world would lighten
and without thinking he would be able to lift
from his back the wings of night
and lift the stones from his teeth
and would be able to speak.
But he could not say that either.
He could do nothing but lie there
and wait for the sun to go down,
wait for the promise of stillness
that would be sent from his heart into the field,
and wait for it to return.
And later he would lie there
and pretend it was morning.
In the dark he would still be uncertain of how to begin.
He would mumble to himself; he would follow
his words to learn where he was.
He would begin.
And the room, the house, the field,
the woods beyond the field, would also begin,
and in the sound of his own voice beginning
he would hear them.

III

THE STORY OF OUR LIVES

THE STORY OF OUR LIVES

To Howard Moss

1

We are reading the story of our lives
which takes place in a room.
The room looks out on a street.
There is no one there,
no sound of anything.
The trees are heavy with leaves,
the parked cars never move.
We keep turning the pages,
hoping for something,
something like mercy or change,
a black line that would bind us
or keep us apart.
The way it is, it would seem
the book of our lives is empty.
The furniture in the room is never shifted,
and the rugs become darker each time
our shadows pass over them.
It is almost as if the room were the world.
We sit beside each other on the couch,
reading about the couch.
We say it is ideal.
It is ideal.

2

We are reading the story of our lives
as though we were in it,
as though we had written it.
This comes up again and again.

In one of the chapters
I lean back and push the book aside
because the book says
it is what I am doing.
I lean back and begin to write about the book.
I write that I wish to move beyond the book,
beyond my life into another life.
I put the pen down.
The book says: *He put the pen down*
and turned and watched her reading
the part about herself falling in love.
The book is more accurate than we can imagine.
I lean back and watch you read
about the man across the street.
They built a house there,
and one day a man walked out of it.
You fell in love with him
because you knew he would never visit you,
would never know you were waiting.
Night after night you would say
that he was like me.
I lean back and watch you grow older without me.
Sunlight falls on your silver hair.
The rugs, the furniture,
seem almost imaginary now.
She continued to read.
She seemed to consider his absence
of no special importance,
as someone on a perfect day will consider
the weather a failure
because it did not change his mind.
You narrow your eyes.

26

You have the impulse to close the book
which describes my resistance:
how when I lean back I imagine
my life without you, imagine moving
into another life, another book.
It describes your dependence on desire,
how the momentary disclosures
of purpose make you afraid.
The book describes much more than it should.
It wants to divide us.

3

This morning I woke and believed
there was no more to our lives
than the story of our lives.
When you disagreed, I pointed
to the place in the book where you disagreed.
You fell back to sleep and I began to read
those mysterious parts you used to guess at
while they were being written
and lose interest in after they became
part of the story.
In one of them cold dresses of moonlight
are draped over the backs of chairs in a man's room.
He dreams of a woman whose dresses are lost,
who sits on a stone bench in a garden
and believes in wonders.
For her love is a sacrifice.
The part describes her death
and she is never named,
which is one of the things

you could not stand about her.
A little later we learn
that the dreaming man lives
in the new house across the street.
This morning after you fell back to sleep
I began to turn pages early in the book:
it was like dreaming of childhood,
so much seemed to vanish,
so much seemed to come to life again.
I did not know what to do.
The book said: *In those moments it was his book.*
A bleak crown rested uneasily on his head.
He was the brief ruler of inner and outer discord,
anxious in his own kingdom.

4

Before you woke
I read another part that described your absence
and told how you sleep to reverse
the progress of your life.
I was touched by my own loneliness as I read,
knowing that what I feel is often the crude
and unsuccessful form of a story
that may never be told.
I read and was moved by a desire to offer myself
to the house of your sleep.
He wanted to see her naked and vulnerable,
to see her in the refuse, the discarded
plots of old dreams, the costumes and masks
of unattainable states.
It was as if he were drawn

28

irresistably to failure.
It was hard to keep reading.
I was tired and wanted to give up.
The book seemed aware of this.
It hinted at changing the subject.
I waited for you to wake not knowing
how long I waited,
and it seemed that I was no longer reading.
I heard the wind passing
like a stream of sighs
and I heard the shiver of leaves
in the trees outside the window.
It would be in the book.
Everything would be there.
I looked at your face
and I read the eyes, the nose, the mouth . . .

5

If only there were a perfect moment in the book;
if only we could live in that moment,
we could begin the book again
as if we had not written it,
as if we were not in it.
But the dark approaches
to any page are too numerous
and the escapes are too narrow.
We read through the day.
Each page turning is like a candle
moving through the mind.
Each moment is like a hopeless cause.
If only we could stop reading.

He never wanted to read another book
and she kept staring into the street.
The cars were still there,
the deep shade of trees covered them.
The shades were drawn in the new house.
Maybe the man who lived there,
the man she loved, was reading
the story of another life.
She imagined a dank, heartless parlor,
a cold fireplace, a man sitting
writing a letter to a woman
who has sacrificed her life for love.
If there were a perfect moment in the book,
it would be the last.
The book never discusses the causes of love.
It claims confusion is a necessary good.
It never explains. It only reveals.

6

The day goes on.
We study what we remember.
We look into the mirror across the room.
We cannot bear to be alone.
The book goes on.
They became silent and did not know how to begin
the dialogue which was necessary.
It was words that created divisions in the first place,
that created loneliness.
They waited.
They would turn the pages, hoping
something would happen.

They would patch up their lives in secret:
each defeat forgiven because it could not be tested,
each pain rewarded because it was unreal.
They did nothing.

7

The book will not survive.
We are the living proof of that.
It is dark outside, in the room it is darker.
I hear your breathing.
You are asking me if I am tired,
if I want to keep reading.
Yes, I am tired.
Yes, I want to keep reading.
I say yes to everything.
You cannot hear me.
They sat beside each other on the couch.
They were the copy, the tired phantoms
of something they had been before.
The attitudes they took were jaded.
They stared into the book
and were horrified by their innocence,
their reluctance to give up.
They sat beside each other on the couch.
They were determined to accept the truth.
Whatever it was they would accept it.
The book would have to be written
and would have to be read.
They are the book and they are
nothing else.

INSIDE THE STORY

1

He never spoke much
but he began to speak even less.
And the chair in the living room was unsafe.
And the bed in the bedroom was never made.
And nothing was the same as it had been.
Still, he said he was happy.
He would look at the stars
and their distance confirmed what he felt.
If there was order, then he was a part of it;
if there was chaos, then it wasn't his fault.
He had no cause for anger.
When he spoke to his wife
the subject was always the same:
she would travel and see the world,
he would stay home and water the plants;
or, he would see the world and she
would water the plants.
Their lives continued.
She undressed in the dark bathroom.
He read a dull book in the kitchen.
Nothing changed until she admitted she loved him;
that night he slept in the living room,
alone, and had a dream.

2

He dreamed that he had gone,
and no one had seen him off.
Under the simple moon

the stones and bushes looked alike.
It was the end of summer and he could smell the grass
and feel the wind from the lake.
He loved farewells. He loved
not knowing where he was going,
and the dark and the deep wind driving him
farther and farther were like desire.
And if his enemies crouched in the moonlight,
he did not notice them,
nor did he notice the owl staring into his limbs,
nor feel the moth pressing against his ribs
as if he were the only light.
And he did not hear the cry that would always be with him,
that rose from his throat like a name
beginning to shape the sound of its being.
He wanted to learn the lessons of dark,
and he wanted the sheets of morning to take him in.
He wanted both, and woke
unable to say the one thing he would try to remember.

3

It was early.
She stood over him, offering him coffee.
She asked him what he was trying to say.
There was no way to tell her what he had not said.
His voice would fail to convey what it was,
and his silence would fail to suggest its absence.
He remembered the driving wind
and the way he waved into the dark
and how the distance kept welcoming him.
He wished she had not asked.

He imagined that he had wakened in the wrong house,
that he would leave, that he would go back.
And he drifted off to sleep.
If he had gone before, he did not know it now.
The clouds moving slowly over the lake,
the failed brilliance of daylight,
seemed too much a part of the present.
He went from field to field,
each one blank with possibility,
each one darkening with disappointment.
As he went he felt the acuteness of his passion.
He walked because he had to,
and when he looked up, the sky was empty
and the world seemed cleared of meaning.
Once again, he tried to say something,
but he awoke.

4

She stood over him.
She said she had watched him,
that he had been trying to say something.
He had nothing to say.
He lay on the couch with his eyes open.
Sometimes he did not know if he slept
or just thought about sleep. He knew
that he would lie down and the journey would begin.
If it was another life, it was not the one which lasted.
He would have to come back
and recapture what he had left.
He would offer himself as hostage
and the life he woke into would take him.

How long would it last?
When he closed his eyes, the clouds had gone,
the sun had turned everything white.
Even if he became less than he was and the terrain
became harsher, even if no trace remained
of his having been, he would keep going.
He felt he had given up the visible world,
that the sun had turned everything white to prepare his way.
He walked in the harsh light,
and when he stopped he discovered
he was standing beside someone who wore clothes like his
and whose face was like his own and who asked,
Where am I? Where am I going?
He tried to answer but the cloud of his voice would say nothing.
He wanted to know who the man was.
He tried to think of his name, but again he woke.

5

She watched him open his eyes
and asked him what he had said about a name.
He tried to remember where he was going.
Was he looking for someone?
The light came in the windows,
erasing the furniture, turning
the room white. He saw nothing.
And he remembered how she would dress and undress
and how he would wait in bed, watching her.
All night he would feel her beside him,
her breathing moved through his dreams
and shook him like nothing else.

He had traveled a great distance since then
and did not know where he was going.
She told him the coffee was getting cold.
He closed his eyes.
The journey was not what he wanted.
Each day was too long, and not long enough
to endure himself in. And there was nothing ahead.
The stranger had gone and there was
no lake or fields or woods.
The sun's brightness fell and he continued,
his ignorance shining, his failure
finding him out and leading him on.
Survival was motion and he could not stop.

6

She sat in a chair across the room, staring at him.
It was not a bad life, he thought
as he sipped the cold coffee
and she moved into a closer chair.
Still, he could not speak.
She would leave the room and change
into a cooler dress, a warmer dress.
She might even take a trip.
She leaned over him. She said she'd been watching him,
was there something he wanted to tell her?
He knew she would meet somebody.
He knew she would leave him.
He tried to tell her to stay but it was no use.
His mouth was dry and the sun was white
and he could not take another step.
He tried to call, but could not remember the name.

36

He stood in the absence of what he had known
and waited, and when he woke
the room was empty. The light had turned
and the chair she had sat in was covered with dust.
He had been gone a long time
and now the journey was over.
Without her he would not be able to sleep,
and there was no more to say,
and even if there were, he would not say it.

THE UNTELLING

He leaned forward over the paper
and for a long time saw nothing.
Then, slowly, the lake opened
like a white eye
and he was a child
playing with his cousins,
and there was a lawn
and a row of trees
that went to the water.
It was a warm afternoon in August
and there was a party
about to begin.
He leaned forward over the paper
and he wrote:

I waited with my cousins across the lake,
watching the grown-ups walking on the far side
along the bank shaded by elms. It was hot.
The sky was clear. My cousins and I stood
for hours among the heavy branches, watching
our parents, and it seemed as if nothing would enter
their lives to make them change, not even the man
running over the lawn, waving a sheet
of paper and shouting. They moved beyond the claims
of weather, beyond whatever news there was,
and did not see the dark begin to deepen
in the trees and bushes, and rise in the folds
of their own dresses and in the stiff white
of their own shirts. Waves of laughter carried

over the water where we, the children, were watching.
It was a scene that was not ours. We were
too far away, and soon we would leave.

He leaned back.
How could he know
the scene was not his?
The summer was with him,
the voices had returned and he saw the faces.
The day had started before the party;
it had rained in the morning
and suddenly cleared in time.
The hems of the dresses were wet.
The men's shoes glistened.
There was a cloud shaped like a hand
which kept lowering.
There was no way to know
why there were times that afternoon
the lawn seemed empty, or why even then
the voices of the grown-ups lingered there.
He took what he had written
and put it aside.
He sat down and began again:

We all went down to the lake, over the lawn,
walking, not saying a word. All the way
from the house, along the shade cast by the elms.
And the sun bore down, lifting the dampness, allowing
the lake to shine like a clear plate surrounded
by mist. We sat and stared at the water and then
lay down on the grass and slept. The air turned colder.

The wind shook the trees. We lay so long we imagined
a hand brushing the fallen leaves from our faces.
But it was not autumn, and some of us, the youngest,
got up and went to the other side of the lake
and stared at the men and women asleep; the men
in stiff white shirts, the women in pale dresses.
We watched all afternoon. And a man ran down
from the house, shouting, waving a sheet of paper.
And the sleepers rose as if nothing had happened,
as if the night had not begun to move
into the trees. We heard their laughter, then
their sighs. They lay back down, and the dark came over
the lawn and covered them. As far as we know
they are still there, their arms crossed over their chests,
their stiff clothing creased. We have never been back.

He looked at what he had written.
How far had he come?
And why had it grown dark just then?
And wasn't he alone when he watched the others
lie down on the lawn?
He stared out the window,
hoping the people at the lake,
the lake itself, would fade.
He wanted to move beyond his past.
He thought of the man
running over the lawn who seemed familiar,
He looked at what he had written
and wondered how he had crossed the lake,
and if his cousins went with him.
Had someone called?

Had someone waved goodbye?
What he had written told him nothing.
He put it away and began again:

I waited under the trees in front of the house,
thinking of nothing, watching the sunlight wash
over the roof. I heard nothing, felt
nothing, even when she appeared in a long
yellow dress, pointed white shoes, her hair
drawn back in a tight bun; even when
she took my hand and led me along the row
of tall trees toward the lake where the rest had gathered,
the men in their starched shirts, the women in
their summer dresses, the children watching the water.
Even then, my life seemed far away
as though it were waiting for me to discover it.
She held my hand and led me toward the water.
The hem of her dress was wet. She said nothing
when she left me with my cousins and joined
the others who stood together. I knew by the way
they talked that something would happen, that some of us,
the youngest, would go away that afternoon
and never find the way back. As I walked through the woods
to the other side of the lake, their voices faded
in the breaking of leaves and branches underfoot.
Though I walked away, I had no sense of going.
I sat and watched the scene across the lake,
I watched and did nothing. Small waves of laughter
carried over the water and then died down.
I was not moved. Even when the man
ran across the lawn, shouting, I did nothing.

It seemed as if the wind drew the dark
from the trees onto the grass. The adults stood
together. They would never leave that shore.
I watched the one in the yellow dress whose name
I had begun to forget and who waited with
the others and who stared at where I was
but could not see me. Already the full moon
had risen and dropped its white ashes on the lake.
And the woman and the others slowly began
to take off their clothes, and the mild rushes of wind
rinsed their skin, their pale bodies shone
briefly among the shadows until they lay
on the damp grass. And the children had all gone.
And that was all. And even then I felt
nothing. I knew that I would never see
the woman in the yellow dress again,
and that the scene by the lake would not be repeated,
and that that summer would be a place too distant
for me ever to find myself in again.
Although I have tried to return, I have always
ended here, where I am now. The lake
still exists, and so does the lawn, though the people
who slept there that afternoon have not been seen since.
And I believe the woman in the yellow dress died.

It bothered him,
as if too much had been said.
He would have preferred
the lake without a story,
or no story and no lake.
His pursuit was a form of evasion:

the more he tried to uncover
the more there was to conceal
the less he understood.
If he kept it up,
he would lose everything.
He knew this
and remembered what he could—
always at a distance,
on the other side of the lake,
or across the lawn,
always vanishing, always there.
And the woman and the others would save him
and he would save them.
He put his hand on the paper.
He would write a letter for the man
running across the lawn.
He would say what he knew.
He rested his head in his arms and tried to sleep.
He knew that night had once come,
that something had once happened.
He wanted to know but not to know.
Maybe something had happened
one afternoon in August.
Maybe he was there or waiting to be there,
waiting to come running across a lawn
to a lake where people were staring
across the water.
He would come running
and be too late.
The people there would be asleep.
Their children would be watching them.

He would bring what he had written
and then would lie down with the others.
He would be the man
he had become, the man
who would run across the lawn.
He began again:

I sat in the house that looked down on the lake,
the lawn, the woods beside the lawn. I heard
the children near the shore, their voices lifted
where no memory of the place would reach.
I watched the women, the men in white, strolling
in the August heat. I shut the window
and saw them in the quiet glass, passing
each time farther away. The trees began
to darken and the children left. I saw
the distant water fade in the gray shade
of grass and underbrush across the lake.
I thought I saw the children sitting, watching
their parents in a slow parade along
the shore. The shapes among the trees kept changing.
It may have been one child I saw, its face.
It may have been my own face looking back.
I felt myself descend into the future.
I saw beyond the lawn, beyond the lake,
beyond the waiting dark, the end of summer,
the end of autumn, the icy air, the silence,
and then, again, the windowpane. I was
where I was, where I would be, and where I am.
I watched the men and women as the white
eye of the lake began to close and deepen
into blue, then into black. It was too late

for them to call the children. They lay on the grass
and the wind blew and shook the first leaves loose.
I wanted to tell them something. I saw myself
running, waving a sheet of paper, shouting,
telling them all that I had something to give them,
but when I got there, they were gone.

He looked up from the paper
and saw himself in the window.
It was an August night
and he was tired,
and the trees swayed
and the wind shook the window.
It was late.
It did not matter.
He would never catch up
with his past. His life
was slowing down.
It was going.
He could feel it,
could hear it in his speech.
It sounded like nothing,
yet he would pass it on.
And his children would live in it
and they would pass it on,
and it would always sound
like hope dying, like space opening,
like a lawn, or a lake,
or an afternoon.
And pain could not give it
the meaning it lacked;
there was no pain,

only disappearance.
Why had he begun in the first place?
He was tired,
and gave himself up to sleep,
and slept where he was,
and slept without dreaming,
so that when he woke
it seemed as if nothing had happened.
The lake opened like a white eye,
the elms rose over the lawn,
the sun over the elms.
It was as he remembered it—
the mist, the dark, the heat,
the woods on the other side.
He sat for a long time
and saw that they had come
and were on the lawn.
They were waiting for him,
staring up at the window.
The wind blew their hair
and they made no motion.
He was afraid to follow them.
He knew what would happen.
He knew the children would wander off,
that he would lie down with their parents.
And he was afraid.
When they turned
and walked down to the lake
into the shade cast by the elms
the children did wander off.
He saw them in the distance,
across the lake, and wondered if one

would come back someday
and be where he was now.
He saw the adults on the lawn,
beginning to lie down.
And he wanted to warn them,
to tell them what he knew.
He ran from the house down to the lake,
knowing that he would be late,
that he would be left
to continue.
When he got there,
they were gone,
and he was alone in the dark,
unable to speak.
He stood still.
He felt the world recede
into the clouds,
into the shelves of air.
He closed his eyes.
He thought of the lake,
the closets of weeds.
He thought of the moth asleep
in the dust of its wings,
of the bat hanging in the caves of trees.
He felt himself at that moment to be
more than his need to survive,
more than his losses,
because he was less than anything.
He swayed back and forth.
The silence was in him
and it rose like joy,
like the beginning.

When he opened his eyes,
the silence had spread, the sheets
of darkness seemed endless,
the sheets he held in his hand.
He turned and walked to the house.
He went to the room
that looked out on the lawn.
He sat and began to write:

THE UNTELLING

To the Woman in the Yellow Dress

MARK STRAND

Mark Strand was born in Summerside, Prince Edward Island, Canada, but has lived most of his life in the United States, where he has taught at various colleges and universities. His previous books of poetry are: *Sleeping with One Eye Open* (1964), *Reasons for Moving* (1968) and *Darker* (1970).